# WHERE DID
# YOU LEAVE
# THE ADMIRAL?

# WHERE DID YOU LEAVE THE ADMIRAL?

LIBBY PURVES &
PAUL HEINEY

*WITH ILLUSTRATIONS BY*
*DES SLEIGHTHOLME*

STANFORD MARITIME
LONDON

Stanford Maritime, Member company of the George Philip
Group, 27A Floral Street, London WC2E 9DP

First published in Great Britain 1987

© Libby Purves and Paul Heiney 1987;
illustrations © J D Sleightholme

Filmset by Tameside Filmsetting, Ashton-under-Lyne, Lancs
Printed and bound in Great Britain by J W Arrowsmith,
Bristol

British Library Cataloguing in Publishing Data

Heiney, Paul
Where did you leave the admiral?
1. Yachts and yachting—Anecdotes,
facetiae, satire, etc.
I. Title    II. Purves, Libby
797.1'24'0207    GV819

ISBN 0-540-07419-5

# CONTENTS

*To JDS*

*He was thoughtful and grave – but the orders
he gave
Were enough to bewilder a crew.
When he cried 'Steer to starboard, but keep her
head larboard!'
What on earth was the helmsman to do?*

*Then the bowsprit got mixed with the rudder
sometimes:
A thing, as the Bellman remarked,
That frequently happens in tropical climes
When a vessel is, so to speak, 'snarked'.*

from *The Hunting of the Snark* by
Lewis Carroll, 1876

# FOREWORD

ONCE UPON A TIME, when Victoria was Queen, when Britannia still ruled the waves and yachtsmen were Gentlemen, things were very different. These haughty owners, members of the Cumberland Fleet or the Royal Yacht Squadron at Cowes, did not struggle with their own dinghies or spend hours trying to unblock their marine lavatories; they had respectful boatmen to row them out to their moorings, and paid hands to polish the brass. But one luxury which they lacked was communication. There was no cheap and cheerful VHF, no Citizens Band or onboard telex or computerized international message services for the owner afloat; there were only Morse lamps and signalling flags.

So every yacht carried a set of signal flags of a properly large size, and kept them pocketed neatly in a canvas flag-roll or mahogany chest; they flapped out their messages wetly in the Solent breezes and fluttered into tatters on long and majestic European cruises.

The trouble was that, although the Navy had produced the Fleet Signal Book by the middle of the nineteenth century, providing a set of codes to cover everything from *England Expects* to *I Am On Fire*, these dignified

Victorian yachtsmen rapidly discovered that they had a whole set of needs and queries which, somehow, the Navy had never seen fit to codify. Suppose a chap needed to borrow some ginger marmalade? Or explain that the little lady was feeling sick? Or ask, with as much urgency as flags can display, where on earth the Admiral had been abandoned? No point closing with your fellow-yachtsman and bellowing requests through a megaphone all the time; with booms of great length, high swaying topmasts, and all that complicated rigging of lanyards and deadeyes to get entangled, you would probably end up with both boats disabled and the marmalade (if not the lady) lost in the drink. No; a new, private set of flag signal hoists had to be invented, to promote communication between club members and avoid laborious spelling-out of words like *chessboard* or *currant jelly*. So invented they duly were.

To avoid confusion with the comprehensive official list of signal codes, the yachtsmen used numeral flags rather than alphabetical. This may have caused a little confusion when replying to hoists like 6258 (OF WHAT VINTAGE?) because if the other yacht replied 1856 it might mean the vintage, or might equally well be an offer of a side of beef; but no doubt the Owners and their sweating sailing-masters managed to make

10

themselves understood even on the wildest nights in the Channel anchorages.

The signals in this book were taken from George Holland Ackers' *Universal Yacht Signals*, published in 1847, and from the earlier *Royal Yacht Squadron Signals* of 1840. Ackers' introduction sternly states that 'It is desirable that all owners of yachts should provide two copies of this book. One for private use, the other for the use of their sailing-masters'; a nifty bit of marketing, which any modern publisher might envy. We have chosen a few dozen of the more revealing signals, and attempted to illustrate them with some historical incidents and notable personalities of that wonderful, confident yachting century. We hope they will take you back to a golden age of impossibly gentlemanly yachting, when Marina was only a character in a minor Shakespeare play, resin was what one rubbed on one's violin-bow, and boatyards still smelt of sawdust and Stockholm tar. In an age where VHF radios natter and shriek their messages across every yacht harbour, we can only marvel at the truly British thoroughness and inimitable style of this Victorian Yachtsman's Code. Perhaps we could even borrow it back again, when the batteries run low. . . .

# 1204 VAPOUR BATH READY AT THE HOUR SHOWN

WHETHER THIS IS A SIGNAL intended for the club to use, to alert a yachtsman to his Turkish-bath's readiness, or a curt instruction for use by the yacht on dropping its anchor, is not clear. What is quite clear is that only a good steam-clean was likely to remove the accumulated grime from a gentleman who had just taken a sporting run to Cherbourg and back. Even by the nineties, the largest and most luxurious yachts were still not all that well-equipped for human cleanliness. They either had no bath, or one set under the floorboards of a cabin, where – according to Atkins's *Memorials of the Royal Yacht Squadron*

All had to bathe in turn, the water coming cold from the sea and emptying into the bilges whence it was pumped out perhaps once a week. Every lady was forbidden to use even seawater soap in these cold baths, and every lady disobeyed; consequently the soap coated the bilges with a greasy slime and the smells of old yachts became extremely strong. Smells were accepted as an inevitable accompaniment of yachting.

# 3387 SEND OFF A GLAZIER TO REPAIR MY SASHES

IF YOU NOT ONLY WENT OUT TO SEA, but spent your time in port holding balls for 300 and dinner-parties for 22 aboard, like Lord Yarborough, there must have been a fair bit of wear and tear. After all, many of the floating palaces of the Victorian aristocracy were better-appointed than a modern house. As one lady said admiringly:

'Many of these beautiful vessels comprehend all the advantages of the most finished "country villa", besides some which are peculiar to themselves. They have all the accommodation of a house, and are free from the inconvenience of a bad neighbourhood, for their site may be changed at pleasure [but see CAN YOU SPARE ME YOUR FIDDLER?]. They have not only the richest, but also the most varied prospects; they are villas free from house duty and window tax; pay neither tithe nor poor rate; are exempt from government and parochial taxes; and have not only a command of wood and water, but may truly be said to possess the most extensive fishery of any house in England'.

Even when the size of private yachts shrank, the magnificence remained. In 1926 there is a description of the yacht *Alice* which positively makes one's mouth water:

The walls are white with light green panels. Bookshelves run the length of the starboard side of the cabin and beneath them are three lockers with lattice-work doors for ventilation, a green upholstered transom with many soft, life-preserver cushions. Across the room there is another transom, more lockers, and a second water-tank. In place of bookshelves one finds a folding berth hidden in the daytime by a pretty green curtain. At the forward end is a mahogany buffet containing all the glass, silver, and table linen. On top of the buffet, there is a lovely brass tea-set which is kept shining like gold. A mahogany table, with folding sides, is thumbscrewed to the floor and is easily movable in case of dancing. At the after end of the cabin is a large chart locker – I personally would prefer a small piano there – and at the forward end, a little green-tiled stove with an open coal-grate, shining brass trimmings and a stovepipe. . .

However, it is good to find that as early as 1884 there was a growing 'underclass' of yachtsmen whose standards and ambitions were far closer to our own. In fact, a fellow calling himself 'Wanderer' published in that year an account of how five impecunious young city chaps got together to buy a yacht called the *Ocean Queen*. Their account has more in common with *Three Men in a Boat* than with the *Memorials of the Royal Yacht Squadron*. They send off one of their number, Smythe, to conclude the sale, and indulge in a pleased fantasy about 'the luxury we had read and heard much about – the silk settees, beautiful panels, and gorgeous hangings of these floating palaces. We dozed and dreamed of amber curtains, satin couches and gilt mirrors; of six stalwart men in open blue jackets and hats with brims turned up rowing us in a beautiful blue boat with cushioned seats. . . .'.

Then they see the *Ocean Queen*, the only yacht they can afford. 'A clumsy-looking boat, about the size of a Brighton wherry . . . a nasty, ugly little fishing boat'. There was no wheel, only 'an iron bar like a pump handle turned sideways, which we presumed was the tiller'. There was no room to pace the deck heroically and no quiet corners for romantic flirtation. Below, there were 'wretched sofas covered in faded chintz'. The only thing they can find to approve of is the 'rather pretty encaustic tiles' around the fireplace. Still, they make the best of it, hire a crew (one of whom spends the voyage dead drunk on the saloon sofa) and eventually get run down by a steamer and sunk because they haven't lit their navigation lights. 'We had had two days sail, during which time the majority of us were seasick, and no end of trouble, at a cost of not less than £400. We took the paltry £100 the Insurance Company offered us, and swore that we could never trust Smythe again. This was the end of the cruise of the *Moonshine*'.

Makes you feel quite at home, really.

## 2316 KEEP AN EYE ON THE BOAT, I FEAR SHE'LL UPSET

HOWEVER CUSHIONED YOU MAY BE from harsh reality aboard your yacht, the dangerous and uncomfortable bit is getting ashore. The really sensible way to come ashore at Cowes in rough weather is to take your yacht up the river a little way. However, this means walking through the vulgarities of the town before reaching the sanctuary of the Castle, clubhouse of the Royal Yacht Squadron. So members always preferred to anchor out in the Roads – in the full swish of the tide – and come ashore at the Castle's own landing-place. In 1883 the stairs and causeway were improved. As a contemporary journalist wrote, with heavy irony:

'The RYS landing place was desperately inconvenient to ladies' maids. At low water it was not nearly so easy to come alongside as it was to draw up at the door of Mr Peter Robinson's shop in Oxford Street in a brougham, and there were some nasty rocks near it which were very much in the way'.

The new stage involved much blasting away of rocks, and cost £3000, a fortune at the time, and the tough male sea-dogs who had opposed it thought it extremely funny

that the Club – due to this expense – was now unable to give a Ball for the troublesome ladies.

Anyway, the new landing-stage was not an unqualified success in all weathers. One fearful day in 1890 or so, 'a boat from Lord Bute's yacht with ladies aboard was upset, Lady Howard of Glossop being thrown into the water'. To make things worse, Lady Howard was the Owner's mother-in-law.

# 9318  I HAVE LEFT A MAN
## BEHIND, WILL YOU
## BRING HIM?

As a rule, it seems to have been paid hands who fell overboard, while making wild lunges for the falls of halyards, or struggling to disentangle two yachts in the course of a race. The most famous incident of an owner falling overboard himself concerns the third Marquess of Waterford. He was the sort of early-Victorian toff who had spent his youth picking fist-fights with butchers and draymen, and delighted in all sorts of mayhem. He painted a toll-bar bright red, put aniseed on the hoofs of a parson's horse and hunted the divine with bloodhounds, put a donkey into a stranger's bed at an inn, and smashed a valuable French clock on the staircase of Crockford's club with a blow of his fist. He also tried to persuade an Irish railway company to set off two engines in opposite directions on the same line, in order that he might witness the smash, for which he promised to pay.

Had he been born a hundred years later and a few classes down, Waterford would clearly have made an excellent football hooligan. But you have to hand it to him for courage. At Cowes, running fast before the wind in his schooner *Gem*, his cap blew off into the sea. 'I won't lose that cap' he exclaimed, and jumped overboard to save it. He was 'only picked up at the last gasp', and lived until 1859 when his horse rolled on him after being put thrice at an impossible fence. 'It was almost a miracle' they said at the time, 'that he lived to be forty-eight'.

# 9123 LADY IS SEASICK

Presumably some were, although they can't have been overly thrilled to have the fact blazoned in flags forty feet above their aching heads. But not all the yachting ladies were flibbertigibbets in openwork shoes and silk stockings, putting up gracefully with a few nights aboard in the Ladies' Cabin in return for the promise of teas and balls ashore. So hats off to the intrepid Mrs Perkins, wife of a London brewer of the 1840's. She 'used her husband's several yachts as if they were barouches or landaus' for paying morning visits. In 1845 she turned up at Cherbourg in one of her yachts to call upon a lady of her acquaintance. They had a chat about new novels and new Irish melodies – sweetly pretty – and Mrs Perkins offered to nip back to England and fetch some of the new songs which were all the rage in London. One morning shortly afterwards, Mrs Perkins turned up again at her friend's in Cherbourg, with the roll of music in her hand.

'You positively must stay and dine with us' said her friend, grateful for this double Channel crossing to fetch the sheet music. But 'Can't indeed, my dear' replied Mrs Perkins with a toss of her head. 'I must be off immediately; I have promised the wife of the British Consul at Cadiz to drop in upon her, and I know she is expecting me'. So off she went back to London via Spain, as insouciantly as most ladies of the period would do a turn around Green Park.

Years later, Anthony Heckstall-Smith adds to this tale: there was Sir Richard Fairey, who was said to 'use his 700-tonner exactly as you or I would use a bicycle'. It puts a fascinating new light on the signal 9563 I SHALL ATTEND MASONS – WILL YOU? Perhaps chaps in Biscay would fly this at one another, before nipping back home for a Masonic Lodge meeting, then back on their way to the Med.

— Lady is seasick —

# 9680 LUMBAGO

Ominously brief. A sufferer might find it irritating to hoist four numeral-flags all the way up his rigging, twingeing all the time, merely in order to say the one word (rather than anything useful like 'Lend me a deckhand' or 'Send Surgeon Instantly'). Perhaps signal 9680 was rarely used by yachtsmen: certainly there are plenty of examples of people who ought by rights to have had lumbago, but didn't. Take Sir Claude Champion de Crespigny, 1847–1935. He had been a reckless steeplechaser, taken on a picador in a bullring, boxed, swum the rapids at Assuan, and crossed the North Sea in a balloon. He once tried to get Blondin to carry him across a tightrope. In his old age, he and Lady de Crespigny added social daring to physical risk, and bathed without permission from the Royal Yacht Squadron's sacred steps (see KEEP AN EYE ON THE BOAT, I FEAR SHE'LL UPSET). The Flag Officers didn't dare to remonstrate with such an old pair of fire-eaters, but weakly recommended a bathing-hut not far away. When one member asked what ruling he would given on bathing from the steps, the Commodore thought deeply and replied 'This is a privilege reserved for members of eighty years of age and over'.

# 1630 BAR IS VERY DANGEROUS

LOTS OF THINGS ARE VERY DANGEROUS, when a chap gets into a philosophical mood and really *thinks* about them. One summer night Sir Hercules Langrishe was drinking coffee with Lord Crawford, looking out over the quiet anchorage where their yachts lay. Lord Crawford pointed to a brightening star and said 'Some day, that star may run into the Earth'. 'I hope to God' exclaimed Sir Hercules, 'we shall be on the starboard tack!'.

## 185 LET OFF STEAM ENTIRELY

QUITE LITERAL. As early as 1843 the Squadron Committee passed a resolution that 'steamers belonging to the Squadron shall consume their own smoke'. We think – although it is hard to be sure – that this was a joke. In 1814 a more serious rule was passed that 'no steamer of less than 100 horse power' should qualify for entry; and by the end of the century, steam yachts had become madly fashionable, although their need for a huge crew of stokers and vast coal-bunkers below decks made them far less comfortable than pure sailing boats. One of the most famous was the 565-ton *Sunbeam*, an auxiliary schooner in which Lord Brassey travelled immense distances, while his wife en-thusiastically scribbled her memoirs. The crew list for their 1876 world cruise numbers thirty-two, in addition to the family; plus four children including a baby, two dogs, various guests, and a Surgeon (there is rather a gloomy signal 2239 CREW OF SHIP IN QUESTION IS VERY SICKLY, but this could clearly never have applied to the Brasseys; although their baby nearly died of croup on a rough, interminable passage from Honolulu

to Yokohama). They carried a sailing-master, crew of two for the gig, a boatswain and a carpenter and a captain of the hold; nine able seamen and three cooks, as well as engineers, firemen, ladies-maid and nurse. A new undercook was recruited in Hong Kong and three firemen in the Middle East: 'Mahomet, Abraham, and Tom Dollar'. Yet despite this fabulous world of grandeur and service, Lady Brassey's diaries read as breezily as anyone's happy cruising memoirs; whether she is buying bantams in Yokohama, mourning the ship's kitten (who fell down the hawse-pipe and drowned), or exclaiming in disgust at the cost of living in Valparaiso:

A three-and-sixpenny Letts's diary costs two dollars and a half (10s), a tall hat costs fifty-eight shillings, and you must pay sixpence each for parchment luggage-labels. . .

Letting off steam was an entirely alarming business. The boiler-tubes kept bursting in the Pacific heat, once three times in two days. Lady Brassey wrote crossly in her journal:

At four a.m. Powell woke us with the announcement that the boiler-tube had again burst, and that we had consequently ceased steaming. Letting off steam and blowing out the boiler made a tremendous noise which aroused everybody in the ship. The constant effort to maintain one's balance, whether sitting, standing or moving about, has been most fatiguing, and the illness of the children has made matters worse. Baby is, I hope, now quite out of danger.

However, she reports tranquilly that the Southern Cross and the Great Bear were shining 'with brilliancy' that night. A woman of great Victorian value.

# 1430 PLAGUE HAS BROKEN OUT AT . . .

OBVIOUSLY, THIS IS INTENDED FOR the adventurous yachtsmen who wandered the world, like the Brasseys. It could save your life, to see a fellow-member flying that one as you passed him in the Indian Ocean. However, it seems to have been nothing but luck if plagues did not break out spontaneously aboard certain yachts (see VAPOUR BATH READY). One boat was so notorious for its filth that Captain Ponsonby of the 7th Fusiliers, a man who lived full-time in his yacht clubhouse, used to say (probably quite often) that it was 'the test of a good telescope to make her out from the shore before you winded her'. As insults go, it seems worth preserving.

# 6419 I CAN STRONGLY RECOMMEND MY WASHERWOMAN

Signals about laundry sometimes assumed a vital importance. In 1884 a lady called Mrs N M Condy published a pamphlet 'Reminiscences of a Yachting Cruise'. A squadron of yachts had cruised in company Westward from Cowes to Plymouth, she herself aboard the cutter *Ganymede*. After being piped aboard and welcomed by a bugler playing 'a deadly struggle between Hearts of Oak and the Roast Beef of Old England', she began cautiously to settle down to the voyage. The owner, J H W P Smith-Piggott, was a stickler for form, and before the yacht had rounded Egypt Point westbound, had sent a signal to the Commodore of onboard disaster. The cook had forgotten the laundry. *Ganymede* requested 'Permission to Part Company', which was granted, and went back for the washing.

# 1384 HAVE YOU ANY GREEN BAIZE TO SPARE?

WHY MIGHT THEY WANT IT? To create a green-baize door to separate the crew's quarters from the Master's? To re-cover a billiard-table without which the yacht's routines simply could not continue? Or possibly for some domestic experiment in designing a new Crew or Members' Uniform? After all, at least one yacht carried a pair of early sewing-machines in the 1890's, and not only for sail repair but for 'the accommodation of repairs to the garments of ship's company and guests alike'.

Certainly the subject of Uniforms was a vexed one for many years. Crews were frequently outfitted in clothes so close to those of the Royal Navy that official eyebrows were raised and cool messages sent to the owners: between those, the cat o'nine tails (see 2540 SHIP'S COMPANY HAVE TIME FOR BREAKFAST) and the proliferation of un-necessary guns, it must be suspected that some owners had unfulfilled fantasies of naval command.

This is confirmed by the original structure of the yatchtsmen's own costumes. The evening dress of the fasionable yacht owner was a short blue coat, white waistcoat, and black tie, the coat bearing a decided relationship to the short-jacket of the Navy. In 1880 most of the men, led by the Prince of Wales, had taken to wearing short jackets barely to the waist (cf. the old joke, 'I can see you're naval'), but a disapproving description said 'they are not suited for use as ballroom apparel by corpulent gentlemen of forty or thereabouts, whom they make to present the appearance of insufficiently clad celestial globes spangled with golden stars'.

# 2540 SHIP'S COMPANY HAVE TIME FOR BREAKFAST, WILL THEY?

IF THE ANSWER SHOULD BE 'NO', there were certain yachts aboard which the Ship's Company would just have to lump it. In the early days of private yachting, many owners preferred their ships to be run on the naval model (after all, they had up to twenty cannon). Lord Yarborough's second *Falcon*, launched amidst a roar of guns on June 10th, 1894, not only looked like one of the HM ships but was kept under the discipline of one. A naval officer was retained as Chief Officer, and the fifty-four choice hands who manned her had, we are assured, voluntarily placed themselves under naval discipline

The honest tars are so well convinced of the impossibility of being properly managed without due sense of the cat o'nine tails, that they voluntarily consented to its lawful application on board, and ere the *Falcon* left Plymouth Sound, all hands cordially signed a paper setting forth the usefulness of a sound flogging in case of extremity, and their perfect willingness to undergo the experiment whenever deemed necessary for the preservation of good order.

# 5231 WHEN WILL DINNER BE READY?

FOOD WAS OFTEN SUMPTUOUS on board, and even more sumptuous ashore. While the intrepid Brasseys were on the other side of the world, spinning out the meat of a South Sea Island pig, the racing set at Cowes managed to keep their yachts pretty well provisioned. Lord Yarborough's *Falcon*, in 1924, was the scene of a dinner-party for 22, comprising six courses. On the following night Yarborough organized a ball aboard for 300 guests. He stood at his gangway from 10 to 11 pm welcoming a steady stream of guests climbing from boats and launches: country-dances, quadrilles and Scotch reels were danced the length of the yacht's deck, and when the guests descended to the three cabins below, at 2 am, they found 'jellies, creams, champagne, fine pineapples, and grapes' laid out like a banquet in a fairy-tale. Instead of carriages at dawn, it was boats at dawn, as they all streamed happily off down the gangway.

# 3641 CAN YOU RECOMMEND ME A SHOEMAKER?

IT WOULD BE A MISTAKE to think that just because they were wealthy gentlemen, Victorian yachtsmen were all smartly turned out. If one of them suddenly needed a shoemaker, it might well have been because his footwear had fallen entirely to pieces from neglect. A newspaper report of a race on the Thames in 1860 waxed eloquent about the heroic and aristocratic aspect of the Cumberland Fleet's club members, then groused 'Their clothes, however, are used-up garments which upon other occasions are stowed away in out-of-the-way clothes bags. . . Why should the gallant spirits who are the thews and sinews of our noblest and manliest national pastime, garb their stalwart forms after such a dubious fashion?'

The picture sounds only too familiar. On the other hand, the matter of shoes could sometimes lead to tensions between gentlemen owners and their visitors. The first Marquess of Anglesey, Lord Uxbridge, is best known as the chap who on the field of Waterloo observed to the Duke of Wellington 'By God, I have lost my leg!', and received the reply 'Have you, by God!'. He

was also a great yachtsman, and extremely proud of the whiteness of the decks of his cutter, *Pearl*. On one occasion he gave a passage to one Lord Adolphus FitzClarence, who wore carefully varnished boots which always left marks on the deck after a shower. Anglesey (who himself, of course, had only the one boot to worry about, and would never have worn a varnished one) detailed off one of his paid hands to follow the offender with a swab, and remove the mark of every footstep. It is not recorded whether Lord Adolphus FitzClarence enjoyed his cruise, or indeed even noticed the grim-faced man permanently behind him with the mop.

Lord Anglesey was, to the last, a great sportsman. When the yachting season was over, he would shoot grouse from a pony. On one occasion he shot through the crown of a tall hat on the head of a Welsh clergyman, who was terrified. 'My good man' remarked Anglesey. 'Don't be afraid, I'm a perfect master of the weapon'.

# 48 OBSERVE THE COMMODORE IN THE NIGHT AS HE MAY ALTER COURSE WITHOUT MAKING SIGNALS

NOT EVERYONE ON THE WATER knew what he was doing and where he was going. Guests, in particular, might be kept severely in the dark about the nature of their outing. One Mr Bentinck delighted to take his friends on a sea voyage with him, but 'could never be induced to give any particulars as to where bound or the probable length of the cruise'. He very much resented any inquiries on the subject. His friends seem to have had a beautiful trust in him, however, and in his yacht *Dream*; they used to 'settle their affairs for a reasonable period, not knowing when they would return'. Or, indeed, whether they would. His favourite trip ever lasted 42 days, from Cowes to Gibraltar; his favourite story was about a Baltic storm where the yacht shipped 'twenty tons of green water'.

After keying themselves up to face almost anything, anywhere, his guests must have been rather let down (if relieved) when he occasionally settled for a brief trip to Weymouth.

# 39 CLOSE NEARER TO THE COMMODORE AND FOLLOW HIS MOTIONS

IN 1886 THERE WAS AN ATTEMPT to revive the dying tradition of splendid, orderly, crypto-Naval 'cruises in company'. The Commodore of the Royal Yacht Squadron led a line of thirteen sailing yachts in the *Aline*, and the Vice-Commodore, Lord Ormonde, followed in the steamer *Santa Maria* with five steam yachts. Manoeuvres were planned. Alas, a contemporary account indicates that the result was not so much a stirring naval sight as a pig's breakfast:

The wind was light, and owing to no sort of system having been adopted with regard to the size and speed of the sailing vessels, the distances were not kept. The Commodore's and Vice-Commodore's yachts and one repeating vessel were supplied with men-o'war's signalmen borrowed from the *Southampton*, but the rest of the yachts displayed an utter ignorance not only of signals but of the means of making and answering them. Near the Nab the whole squadron ran into a thick fog, and for an hour no-one could see anything. At 4 pm the fog cleared, and the

squadron, which was discovered in great confusion, all their sails anyhow, was twice ordered to 'tack instantly'. As, however, the signal as made was 'tack gravely', there was some natural doubt as to what was meant.

The full horror of this occasion can only be comprehended when you remember that the Nab Tower is in full telescope's-view of Portsmouth, and also of the summer resort of Bembridge. The account concludes:

It is devoutly to be trusted that at some early period the RYS will borrow a sailor or two from somewhere, and will vindicate its high pretensions and do credit to its white ensign by having a cruise at least ten miles out at sea, or naval evolutions properly performed, or perhaps even both

At a hundred years' distance, you can feel their ears burning.

# 531 YOUR NUMBER IS FLYING AT THE CLUBHOUSE

As YACHT CLUBS GOT MORE ORGANIZED, they used to summon members for messages by individual numbers. There was also rather a charming habit of wishing cruising members good luck and a prosperous voyage, by hanging a personal message from the club yardarm. This had the power to cause some embarrassment in timid yachtsmen. The owner of the *Laverock* announced once that he proposed to cruise to the West Country from the Solent, and filled the days with ostentatious preparations. But no sooner had she left than a nasty contrary wind sprang up and sent her slinking back to her mooring. The Club raised a new signal: 'Welcome Home, *Laverock*!'.

# 3482 I WANT A CARRIAGE AT THE HOUR SHOWN

Some noble yachtsmen lived lives of extreme splendour and wasteful eccentricity, and didn't have to order hackney carriages, their own being always on standby. Lord Lonsdale (see I am afraid of being taken aback) was a great friend of the Kaiser, lived in feudal splendour at Lowther and kept up a fleet of bright yellow carriages and motor-cars. Some thought him a touch vulgar, and he was at first blackballed for the Squadron. The story goes that he had just bought a huge steam yacht called *Finlandia* to entertain his friend the Kaiser, but then found himself rejected. He immediately telegraphed the yacht broker and cancelled the purchase, then hastened down to Cowes (presumably in a bright yellow carriage) and harangued the Committee in strong language. How was he supposed to entertain a Royal Guest with no yacht and no club? It is one of the few occasions in the club's history when it caved in.

The Kaiser asked him back, to Kiel Regatta in 1904. Lonsdale was met by a fully-uniformed Guard of Honour composed of senior naval officers. He stepped ashore wearing a panama hat, a bright yellow waistcoat, white hunting stock, and black and white striped trousers, with a huge cigar in his mouth. He handed his suitcase to the nearest officer (who happened to be a German Admiral) and strode up the jetty smoking nonchalantly. War did break out, but not for another ten years.

# 127 MEMBERS REQUESTED TO ATTEND GENERAL MEETING IMMEDIATELY

No smouldering cannonball ever fired can have caused as much social devastation as the black balls used in ballots by gentlemen's clubs to indicate that a prospective member was 'not suitable' in some way.

On the face of it, the ballot seems a fair system of holding an election. Potential members' names are announced, and should any existing member feel for any reason that this is not a suitable man to have as a member, he merely has to cast his blackball in the ballot and that will be the end of the matter.

It was a civilised way of holding an election. It was also a rogue's charter; a *carte blanche* for any crusty old rascal to exclude anyone from the company simply because he did not like the cut of his jib.

In the case of the smarter and more exclusive yacht clubs, where membership said more about your position in society than mere ownership of a luxury yacht could, the blackballing was a vicious and cruel business. It was made more bloody by the natural conservatism of the existing members, who, having been elected, were quite happy to pull up the drawbridge on anybody else.

One senior member of the Royal Yacht Squadron (taking notice of the weather like a duck might before laying an egg) is said to have always cast a blackball when the wind was in the east. Another member used his blackball whenever someone came up for election with the same initials as him. He had no intention of allowing any confusion over the initialled hat-pegs.

Fame and fortune were not guarantees of membership either. When the eminent Earl of Cardigan, hero of the Battle of Waterloo, came up for election, his success in the ballot was far from certain. As the *Sporting Magazine* at the time noted,

Some time ago, a gallant Earl who has attracted a good deal of notice in his military capacity was proposed for ballot as a member and duly blackballed. His proposers and friends took fierce umbrage at this, and threatened to blackball everyone that should in future go for election, no matter who it should be. Now, as one blackball in ten does the business, a score or so could hold the Electoral Thermopylae against the whole force of the society brought together at its quarterly meetings.

The *Sporting Magazine* seems to have revelled

in bringing to the public notice the way in which the blackballs ricocheted around Cowes at election time. Most of the stories that appeared were from the pen of an enigmatic 'JBG' who the official historian of the Squadron describes as 'fertile'. Detecting a hint of party politics creeping into the blackballing, he wrote:

There were only two cases of blackballing in the old days: one of a Duke – Buckingham – who did not renew his subscription, and was rejected on seeking re-election; the other the owner of a yacht like a river barge with a flat bottom, and he was excluded more in joke than otherwise, it being reported that she was two months in her voyage from the Thames to Cowes, and that moreover, *the bulkhead and chimney in the cabin were of brick*. But this was not done for party reasons.

And so it is quite clear why such urgency is implied in this signal; why members should 'immediately' report to the clubhouse. Who knows who might be wishing to join their company. S'truth, he might be an eminent war hero, or an innocent old boy who just likes to take things steady as he cruises down Channel. Pass the blackball, Henrietta.

# 1068  I WILL THANK YOU TO LEAVE YOUR ADDRESS WITH ME

THESE DAYS, IT'S THE ADDRESS of your insurance company. Whether the racing yachts of the great days were ever insured is unlikely. The early cup races resulted in extensive damage every time. The *Sporting Magazine* reports on a needle-match between the *Harriet*, the *Miranda* and the *Arrow*, over eighty miles. A sudden tack by Arrow across Miranda's bow resulted in a wrangle:

The two vessels became entangled, and a scene of much violence took place from the excitement of the different crews, blows being exchanged. The gallant Sir James Jordan had a narrow escape from a dreadful blow aimed at the back of his head by one of Mr Weld's men with a handspike as the two vessels were touching each other. He avoided the blow by ducking his head, and hitting out right and left, floored the rascal with such tremendous violence that Captain Lyons told me he thought he was done for. Finding, however, at the end of twenty minutes that the *Harriet* had got, by means of their falling foul, considerably ahead, the *Miranda* dropped astern as the only means of extrication, by which the *Arrow* gained nearly a quarter of a mile.

However, justice prevailed and *Miranda* won the Cup. The owners presumably paid for their own damage.

— I will thank you to leave your address with me —

# 4106 COMMODORE WISHES TO SEE YOU

Even the Commodore of the most prestigious Yacht Club in the world is not all-powerful when he comes up against the law. It is time to tell a more modern story: the stirring tale of Niçois the Parrot. This bird went for a cruise aboard the yacht *Andria* to the Mediterranean in 1930, with the Commodore and his wife, Lady Magdalen. While they were away, a severe attack of psittacosis broke out at home, infecting human beings from parrots, and the Ministry of Health ruled that all parrots arriving in British waters from aboard must be destroyed.

Consternation! Lady M had had the parrot Niçois since 1914 (she bought him on a stop at Nice) and he had never been away from her. He had never been ashore or met a foreign bird, but the law was the law, and despite then sending an envoy to the Ministry to plead his case, Niçois was condemned to death. Drastic measures were taken. Commodore and then Lady disembarked at Barcelona and hurried back overland, leaving Niçois on board with the Steward. The Commodore went to Cowes to await the yacht, the lady buried her grief in a cottage in

Anglesey. When the letter came saying Niçois and the yacht were home, and an official had confirmed the death sentence, she shook herself out of grief and telegraphed 'Have nothing done till you receive my letter'. She had formulated a plan: she would write to the Minister of Health herself, while her husband would write to Ramsay MacDonald, and references would be taken from members that the Commodore could be trusted to tell the truth about Niçois' lack of shore-leave.

It was the lady's letter to the Minister of Health that swung it. Nobody knows exactly what she said. But a week later, the parrot was enthroned in triumph on a table in the Squadron garden, holding a levée. He was still alive ten years later.

# 1407 SEVERAL PIRATES ARE CRUISING, LOOK OUT

Most of the early Royal Yacht Squadron vessels had guns of some sort; and all carried a fearsome array of pistols and cutlasses to fend off pirates (the cutlasses also came in useful for slashing the rigging of adversaries during races, a tactic denied to modern racing crews). But many went further: in the early 1860s 'an eccentric person', universally known as The Pirate, is reported to have fallen foul of the Club's disdainful members and been blackballed. His ship was a 150-ton schooner with black sides pierced for sixteen brass cannon. The man convinced himself that one Sir Percy Shelley had caused his rejection, and one summer evening he anchored off the clubhouse, Cowes Castle, and sent a boat ashore with a note saying that unless the piratical owner got an apology within half an hour, he would open fire on it. Sir Percy was not inclined to take much notice, but a fellow-member assured him that the Pirate was 'quite deranged enough to attempt a bombardment', and that although he would certainly be caught and perhaps hanged for it, it really was not worth the trouble and damage. So the marauder got his apology, dipped his ensign, and sailed peacefully away. Infuriatingly, nobody seems to know whether there was any sequel.

There is a signal which the Clubhouse could have hoisted, if it was not quite clear as to his intentions: a simple 3708: HAS THE SIEGE COMMENCED?

— Several pirates are cruising, look out —

# 814 AMMUNITION IS NEARLY EXPENDED

PLENTY OF EARLY YACHTS carried arms, with good reason. Even in this century the White Ensign, being a naval symbol as well as a Squadron one, sometimes attracted actual fire. An extraordinary letter from Lord Ormonde to his members in 1912 tells the story of a yacht lent to an outsider, which had erroneously flown the white ensign to which only the real owner was entitled, when it was being fired on by an Italian destroyer for no clear reason. This led to a remonstrance from the Italian to the British government 'which might have led to grave international difficulty with a friendly Power'. The moral drawn that nobody but members should ever fly the Ensign.

Whether we are to conclude from this that it was OK for international incidents to be sparked off by members of the Squadron, but by no-one else, or that it is quite correct for the warships of 'friendly Powers' to sink British yachts provided no members of the Squadron are on board, remains an impenetrable mystery.

# 9691 CAN YOU LEND ME A TOMAHAWK?

A PRUDENT YACHT carried an axe (as we carry wire-cutters) to sever its own rigging in case of a dismasting. However, these instruments had other uses. There seems to have been a lot of chopping in the heat of the moment during early cutter-races. In 1829 the crew of the *Louisa* calmly went onto their bowsprit and cut the earing of the *Lulworth* from the boom after the other boat tacked across her; the stewards' ruling on the matter later was that 'the use of axes was unjustifiable and unnecessary, since there was neither risk nor danger'. However, *Louisa* got the Cup because the other boat had tacked illegally. There was a lot of dissent. Lord Belfast, in the ensuing discussions, declared that if any vessel on the larboard tack tried to cross him on starboard, he would 'cut her in two'. Two other members replied by announcing their intention of never sailing in any race in which Lord Belfast had a boat entered, except the Ladies' Challenge Cup, 'which they had no intention of leaving to him'. In the columns of the *Hampshire Telegraph*, his Lordship replied that he was very glad to hear it, and so on.

# 1000 I AM AFRAID OF BEING TAKEN ABACK

A PERFECTLY USEFUL SIGNAL for someone with a vast gaff cutter trussed up like a chicken with preventers and running dead before the wind or very close up to it. A gybe or uncontrolled tack with the jib aback could be the end of your mast. But in the more colloquial sense, there was plenty to set a man back in the complex social rituals of shore life. On the 80th anniversary of the Royal Yacht Squadron, for instance, a vast and pompous portrait of all the members was painted, showing them standing in forcedly casual attitudes on the terrace in front of the Castle. There is a mysterious empty space next to the Kaiser: it was originally occupied by the Earl of Lonsdale, a bit of a lad (see I WANT A CARRIAGE). But it was subsequently decided that he didn't deserve such a senior position, and the Committee actually ordered him to be painted out. He reappears near the entrance by the steps, but a keen restorer could probably trace his ghostly outline still lurking at the Kaiser's side.

# 5926 VESSEL IN SIGHT LOOKS LIKE AN ENEMY

THERE WERE REAL ENCOUNTERS with enemies during the century: one Squadron yacht became very closely embroiled in the last moments of the *Alabama* in the Western Channel. But between sportive young men in smaller yachts there was also a certain amount of mock-battle and horseplay. Shooting aboard was a favourite sport: gulls, curlews, and numbers of fairly inedible birds were potted by yachtsmen. When there were no birds around, the game was to shoot down a bottle hung on the end of your own bowsprit. One author reflects 'It is not so easy to break a bottle attached to the end of this spar by a line two foot long as might be supposed. The yacht pitches or rolls, and the bowsprit does not seem to bob with the yacht, so although the distance is absurdly short, there are more misses than hits'. They used to drink a lot of liquor during these sessions, and frequently fall overboard. Another, even more hair-raising sport was for two yachts to try and shoot bottles hanging from the end of *one another's* bowsprits – on a tossing sea the mind recoils at the thought . . .

## 4831 WHAT TIME DOES THE BALL COMMENCE?

LOOKING AT THE GRANDEUR of the latter-day Cowes Week balls, it is pleasing to remember that they had their distinctly dodgy moments in the early days. One was cancelled because they'd spent all the money on a new landing-stage; there were endless complicated wrangles about what was the correct dress, and whether brass buttons on mess-dress were acceptable; and in 1844 the annual regatta ball ceased to be a public event after a disgraceful incident in which two men (giving the names of Watkin and Howard) were discovered calmly picking the pockets of the male guests.

# 3081  CAN YOU SPARE ME YOUR FIDDLER?

YACHTS' COMPANIES OFTEN INCLUDED MUS-
ICIANS – one owner grumbled at the lack of
room provided by the designer for a second
pianoforte – so this signal was at least as
necessary as the ones designed to cadge
redcurrant jelly or chessboards. But in a
curious incident just before the First World
War, the signal might well have been used in
its other sense: with 'spare me', meaning 'let
me off'. Sir John Burgoyne was aboard his
yacht in Cowes Roads when a small schooner
brought up close to him. It showed the ensign
of the Royal Cork Yacht Club (which is
actually older than any British club, to the
great annoyance of these). Early in the
morning, Sir John was aroused by a band
playing a 'blaring and discordant' tune. Well,
it was discordant to him: it was probably just
Celtic. The band was aboard the Irish yacht.
The next morning, the same thing happened
even louder. Burgoyne complained to the
owner, but got no joy: he was told it was the
custom of the ship and the master himself
had provided his crew with the offending
fiddles and pipes. On the third day, the
Englishman fled to Weymouth. The next

morning the same abominable noise awoke him: the Irishman had followed on. He moved on round Portland Bill and right across Lyme Bay to Torquay, and the Irish yacht caught up with him there, still fiddling with each dawn. The same happened at Dartmouth, and when he fled on Westward round Start Point, they met him at Plymouth. It was a persecution. Some of the other heroes chronicled in this book would undoubtedly have set about the enemy with a tomahawk, if not a stomach-pump: but the mild Sir John merely fled back to Cowes and abandoned his yacht until they had gone.

One gets the impression that Sir John Burgoyne was a particularly good man to play tricks of this nature on. There is a pleasing streak of pomposity about the tales: he was the man who blackballed a nervous candidate who had greeted him with the jovial words 'How pleasant it is to see an old Cowes face'. And he was exceptionally keen on the traditions and honourable standing of the Royal Yacht Squadron, and made it his duty to report all infringements to the Committee. One evening, for instance, he informed an officer that a visitor was doing a dreadful thing: standing on the clipped, sacred Castle lawn *with his arm around a lady's waist!* Alas, a closer scrutiny revealed that the man was leaning against the sundial.

— Can you spare me your fiddler? —

# 6282 COME AND HAVE A RUBBER OF WHIST

# 1747 CAN YOU SPARE A PACK OF PLAYING-CARDS?

# 2960 CAN YOU LEND ME A CHESSBOARD?

It would be a dignified and delightful thought to imagine these well-conducted gentlemen playing at Whist and Loo, or puzzling quietly over chess, during the long evenings out at anchor. No doubt some of them did: but rowdier diversions were also frequent. One owner passed the time shooting the eyes out of his family portraits, alone, with a bottle at his side. A more sociable type was Count Edmund Batthyany, who in the 1870's would bring his guests across the Solent in a barge towed by a tug, or else in his steam yacht *Blunderbuss*, and organize rowdy games of polo aboard hobby-horses. He is also credited with sending up a fire-balloon with an effigy of Lord Beaconsfield on it (it crashed on the beach) and another one of Mr Gladstone. The chronicle says that Gladstone, whose

Whigs were doing well that year 'went sailing away over the Solent, occasionally, as the wind freshened, making most graceful salutations to his admirers ere he disappeared over the purple hills of the Isle of Wight'. After a few parties like that, presumably the playing-cards and chess-board would seem rather tame.

# CAN YOU LEND ME:
## 2857 ALE X QUARTS

## 2895 ALE (PALE), BOTTLES OF

## 2905 BRANDY (BEST)

## 2906 BRANDY (COMMON)?

THERE SEEMS TO HAVE BEEN a great deal of friendly borrowing between yachts. Or was it always so friendly? Lord Anglesey spoke contemptuously of freeloaders, even in prosperous 1850 – chaps 'cruising for cutlets'. And the above list might suggest that anyone spotting the numeral flag '2' on its way up a hoist would do well to tack rapidly and put the telescope to his blind eye: things could get expensive. Especially as the yacht clubs grew in size through the century. A resolution at the Royal Yacht Club was passed in 1816 to the effect that 'although many members are not personally acquainted, it is hoped that no introduction to each other will be deemed necessary in any case where assistance or otherwise may be required, but that any communication by signal may be always received with that cordiality which it was the first object of the club to establish, although the parties may be personally unacquainted'.

In other words, if you spot anyone wearing the same flag as you, you are entitled, if equipped with a copy of Ackerman's yacht signals, to badger him unmercifully for ale, brandy, Madeira wine (3285), and even a bottle of 7065 (CHERRIES, BRANDIED) or 8095 (CAN YOU SPARE ME A HOGSHEAD OF BEER?). If he should hoist NO, you can always come back with a more moderate request, 7132 (CAN YOU SPARE SOME YEAST?), and start the process of brewing your own; but with luck, he will take the Club's advice to heart, and merely grit his teeth and hoist 6258 (OF WHAT VINTAGE?). It is to be hoped that during this frenzied exchange, neither of you is dragging his anchor.

# 3785 THE SIGNAL MADE IS NOT IN MY BOOK

IT WOULD BE A GRAVE MISTAKE to assume that because the signal books exist, everyone knew them and used them properly. Appalling misunderstandings cropped up all the time, and totally unlisted signals would occasionally be hoisted (like that invented by Sir Thomas Lipton, who on being blackballed for the Squadron, threatened to anchor off it flying a hoist of MOBYC – My Own Bloody Yacht Club). Etiquette and entitlement were particularly jealously guarded. One poor devil got blackballed merely for having ordered RYS to be engraved on the rudder-head of his new yacht before he was actually elected – it was considered presumptuous. By the end of the century, pomp and tribal self-importance at Cowes had become stifling, and plenty of fierce blimps with binoculars would be standing by to leap on any breach of regulations. On one occasion someone spotted a boat sailing around with the flag of the Warden of the Cinque Ports at the main, the standard of the Vice-Admiral of Ulster at the Mizzen, and the White Ensign at the peak. And all this within a hundred yards of the Royal Yacht

*Britannia* with Queen Victoria herself aboard! Apoplectic with fury, the spotter alerted the naval guardship, which put down a boat to go across and deal with this frightful cad – but luckily someone checked the reference books, and found that the yachtsman must be Lord Dufferin (see DOES THE PRODUCE COME FROM THE OTTOMAN EMPIRE?) who was – as Lord Warden and Vice-Admiral of Ulster and a Royal Yacht Squadron member – fully entitled to all three flags. So there.

# 9719 CAN YOU SPARE A SOUP TUREEN?

THE SAGA OF MRS CONDY'S CRUISE CONTINUES. The wind freshened just as dinner was being served. The yacht heeled. The table was of the fully-swinging variety, so when the nervous guest grabbed it, her host ordered her harshly to 'Let go!' – before all the dishes could slide off. Since the floor and chairs were not gimballed – you can't have everything – Mrs Condy writes:

'I was now compelled to continue my repast in a most decidedly uncomfortable manner, the table being exactly on a level with my nose. The nearest approach to my position which I can describe, would be sitting on a footstool, hopelessly endeavouring to dine with comfort off the chimney-piece'.

Between swinging tables and non-swinging guests, it becomes painfully obvious why yachts carried one, if not several, spare soup tureens as a matter of course.

# 1856 AM GOING TO SEND FOR BEEF, DO YOU WANT ANY?

GETTING AND KEEPING FRESH MEAT before the advent of tins was a tiresome business, hence the presence on deck of many crates of fowls (see YOUR ZEAL HAS BEEN NOTICED and CURRANT JELLY). The advent of tinned meat was a godsend. General J B Sterling is a yachtsman after our own hearts: he died in 1926 after an adventurous life in the Guards (he invented a special way to rescue General Gordon at Khartoum, but they wouldn't let him try it) and fifty-five years' yachting in his *Juliet*, *Chanticleer*, *Raven*, and *Iris*. These gradually decreased in size, from 118 tons down to 60; and his last boat was an 18-ton cutter, *Chough*, in which he sailed alone for long distances both North and South. He was not a great man for fresh meat: Sterling 'was reputed to regulate the length of his cruises entirely by the amount of corned beef which he could carry. His rule was to return for more whenever the supply ran short'. They called him Sinbad the Sailor.

# 2285 CAN YOU SPARE ME A LITTLE CURRANT JELLY?

———⧫◇⧫———

THE 'CAN YOU SPARE ME' (as opposed to the haughty 'Send off', e.g. in 5354 SEND OFF X BOTTLES OF MIXED PICKLES) implies that one owner was borrowing off another in some foreign anchorage. Pickles and jellies play a large part in the signal-book, no doubt because of the monotony of the pre-refrigerator diet. Before tins were perfected as a means of storing food (see 1856 AM GOING TO SEND FOR BEEF), the only reliable way to ensure a supply of fresh meat was to keep a crate of cockerels and hens on board. Apart from disrupting religious services, as in the case of the yacht *Anona* (see YOUR ZEAL HAS BEEN NOTICED), these were the target of many merry pranks. One yacht's hands would release another yacht's fowls over-night, preferably down the nearest hatch. The chickens' habit of early waking was a great nuisance, and on one occasion the crew of a yacht grew so weary of being woken at dawn by the crowing of the cockerel that the boy who fed the fowls tried the experiment of soaking their corn in gin to stupefy them. It didn't work. The birds 'awoke next morning like giants refreshed, an hour earlier than usual, crowing with renewed vigour'. The currant jelly no doubt overtook them in the end, though.

— Can you spare me a little currant jelly? —

# 5065 DOES THE PRODUCE COME FROM THE OTTOMAN EMPIRE?

THIS SEEMS A TRIFLE FUSSY, considering it is one of the group of signals for borrowing food and drink, but someone must have felt the need for a specific signal to check up on the provenance of dates or saffron-stalks. In some cases, produce might well have travelled from the Ottoman Empire in the very yacht that stored it: adventurous spirits like Lord Dufferin, former Viceroy of India, made tremendous voyages to the Eastern Mediterranean and (in 1856) to Iceland. He was, in fact, once Ambassador to Constantinople and used to sail alone around there in a boat of his own design. *The Times* tells how, at a critical point in diplomatic negotiations which culminated in the British occupation of Egypt in 1882, he was urgently called to the Palace. He sauntered up in his yachting clothes, which greatly impressed the Sultan with his unconcern and British cool.

Lord Dufferin was an unusual yachtsman for the mid-19th century, because his favourite form of sailing was to singlehand small boats. He had a little yawl fitted with every sort of contrivance for handling her from the cockpit – you could even cat the anchor without going forward. A friend once noticed him sailing alone in the middle of the Solent, hove-to on the starboard tack, and fast asleep. He loved the theatre, and would sail from Cowes to Southampton, see a play, and afterwards sail back home to Cowes.

# 4052 CAN YOU SPARE SOME SOUP?

A NATURAL SEQUEL TO 9719, CAN YOU SPARE A SOUP TUREEN? If the tureen is gone, so, presumably, is the soup. But note also 2285 CAN YOU SPARE ME A LITTLE CURRANT JELLY? 5384 SEND OFF X BOTTLES OF MIXED PICKLES; 5521 SEND OFF A HUNDRED PRAWNS.

It is interesting that all the signals relating to alcoholic drinks begin CAN YOU LEND ME, whereas CAN YOU SPARE (for food) implies that you'd never think of returning food to a fellow-gentleman. The SEND OFF signals were clearly to be addressed to minions and club stewards ashore. If the recipient of the signal reckoned you deserved help, his reply would be a polite, but curiously cautious: 4091 I THINK I CAN SPARE YOU SOME.

Even then, the cooking might be a problem. Yachts tended to inherit some of the professional deep-sea cooks: their communal title, given by clipper-men, was 'Old Slush'. The traditional attitude was that strong men could eat anything. Lucky was the nobleman who managed to bring one of his shoreside cooks onto his yacht, and keep him upright enough to concoct something edible borrowed from fellow-members.

# 7159 YOUR ZEAL HAS BEEN NOTED

ON A WELL-ORDERED OCEANGOING YACHT like the great *Sunbeam*, no Sunday passed (even in terrible weather) without 'Litany at 11 and Service with a sermon at 4'. In dire conditions, the sermon was dispensed with. Lesser yachts, whose owners could quite well go ashore to worship, were well-advised not to bother with onboard services. Witness the humiliating experience of Mr Matsell, of the yacht *Anona*. He had a burning ambition, which was part religious and part social, to hold a full naval-style Church Parade and morning service aboard his craft. He attempted this one day in Weymouth Harbour. As was usual, several neighbouring craft carried crates of live fowls on deck to ensure a supply of fresh meat, and one carried a French guest called Antoine. A neighbouring yachtsman delivered the following report on the stirring events of Sunday morning; it would be impossible to better it, so here it is verbatim.

On board a man-of-war, when service is being performed, the church pennant is always hoisted at the peak. Now a cutter has no peak when the mainsail is furled, so there was nothing for it but to hoist the mainsail, for I

am convinced he would have considered the whole ceremony invalid had not this important little piece of bunting been displayed to tell heaven what we were at. Accordingly, up went the peak, out flew the flag, and roll, roll went the *Anona*, puzzled to know why her wings were spread after this strange fashion. The captain and crew were summoned: some of them looked cross, others inclined to laugh, but all of us tried our best to appear composed and decorous, as we ought to be on this occasion. But just as the first few prayers were concluded (amongst which Mr Matsell said with most impressive gravity the prayer for all who were at sea, particularly the Squadron), off came a squall from the shore, flap went the mainsail, creak went the deck, and down went our little French friend Antoine, muttering an unholy *sacré*! Away went the captain's tarpauling hat, which he had been permitted to retain on the plea of being distracted with the rheumatics. Whisk, it flitted its way through many hands outstretched to save it, and settling on the briny element, walked away astern. . .

This was not the end of the story. Antoine described a full somersault, which made the younger element aboard hysterical with laughter, the cockerel and chickens joined in and 'rushed around their crate adding their cackle to the chorus'. The narrator looked at Mr Matsell, hoping in vain for a smile, but met a face of thunder: the hapless owner, surrounded by gales of laughter and the crowing of the cockerel, called out furiously 'Boatswain! Pipe down and be d--d!', to which the Boatswain, controlling his mirth, responded with a very solemn 'Amen'. Thus, concludes our source, 'ended the first and last morning service on board the *Anona*'.

# 4573 WHERE CAN I BORROW
## A STOMACH-PUMP?

EDWARDIAN APPETITES never cease to amaze, especially German appetites. Step forward Baron von Eckhardstein of the German Embassy, an enormous man of enormous capacity who kept a small converted fishing-boat on the Solent at the turn of the century. He used to spend the winter dredging for oysters, which were plentiful, and one night brought eight dozen ashore with him, and ate the lot. When asked by a lady 'Baron, what will you have for breakfast?' he replied 'I generally have som porridge, som fish, som eggs, som cotlets, and there are always de cold meats on de sideboard!'

# 5502 CAN YOU SPARE SOME DINNER-PLATES?

THESE COULD EITHER HAVE DEPARTED SUD-
DENLY from a swinging mahogany dining-
table (see CAN YOU SPARE A SOUP TUREEN?), or
– a more intriguing prospect – they could
have been silver-plate, like those belonging to
Mr George Robert Stephenson of the iron
yacht *Titania*. In 1852 he left her at her
mooring without a watchkeeper, but with a
roaring fire in the cabin. She burned merrily,
and 'all Mr Stephenson's plate was reduced
to two bucketfulls of molten silver'. Mir-
aculously, the 200lb of gunpowder in her
magazine did not explode.

# 3285 MADEIRA WINE

Enthusiastic yachtsmen sometimes never laid up at all. In the 1880's, 'Wanderer' writes, some would bring their boats up the Thames to Erith or Greenhithe, and live aboard all winter. 'They put on dress clothes and go to the play, just catching the last train down at Charing Cross. They often attend evening parties or balls, and seldom ask their friends for a bed, as a cabman can be generally found willing to drive any distance at any hour for sufficient remuneration'. One man owned an old thirty-tonner ballasted with iron, and lived permanently aboard. But on the occasion of a wine sale, at which a good deal of fine Burgundy, Madeira and champagne was knocked down cheap, this man bought a good many dozen bottles and decided to get rid of his iron ballast 'which was lumbering up his vessel and occupying a quantity of room which might have been better employed'. So he took up the floors, threw out the iron pigs, and created a cellar: 130 dozen bottles. 'It was asserted that the vessel was afterwards not in such good trim; but whatever truth there may be in this assertion, it cannot be gainsaid that my friend was in very good trim indeed until all the

hundred and thirty dozen had been con-
sumed'.

He 'kept sparkling Moselle to port,
champagne and Burgundies amidships'. Very
tidy and convenient. However, as he drank
his way through the stock, the boat still
needed ballast; so he ordered his steward to
refill each with sea-water and cork it up. The
steward was a thorough man, and sealed the
bottles as well. The inevitable happened: one
night be served a group of friends 'a tawny
liquid which they did not appear to be
enjoying to any extraordinary extent'. It was
seawater.

This same owner used to hold sing-songs
round his piano, to the disgust of his
neighbours on the moorings, who threatened
to report him to the Thames Conservancy.

## 9018 WILL YOU KEEP NEAR ME DURING THE NIGHT?

## 9108 HAVE YOU A LADY ON BOARD?

THESE MUST HAVE BEEN distressingly easy to confuse, at dusk when the flags were all wet and cold. Anyway, they probably sent up the poor ladies rotten by hoisting 9018 and getting them to say 'Oh yes' to it. Lady guests on yachts (as opposed to lady skippers, see 9123 LADY IS SEASICK) have been teased ever since time began. It is something to do with the enforced, titillating but frustrating lack of privacy on board. It was considered before the First World War that 'sailing yachts under 50ft were unsuitable for cruises with the female sex aboard, because the ladies could not be guaranteed their privacy'. These days, they have to go to sea on 22-footers, and be groped accidentally on purpose by everyone on their way forward to the heads.

*There was a young girl called Bianca*
*Asleep on a ship while at anchor;*
*But she woke in dismay,*
*When she heard the mate say,*
*Let's haul up the top'sheet, and spanker.*

It is very difficult to find romantic passages in the posher end of yachting literature at this time. Ladies appear to be either Amazons or delicate fusspots. But in a fine volume called *Hunt-Room Stories* and *Yachting Yarns*, by a foxhunting yachtsman who appears to live entirely for pleasure, there is a lyrical description of a night passage with a sweet Neapolitan fisher-song wafting across, and:

the couple near the companion-way, perhaps exchanging vows to be confirmed under another vault, more confined than that of the starry heavens above. No wonder, for the air is soft and full of love, and there are no indiscreet eyes to peer under the shadow of the mainsail. . . If warm lips are kissed, what then? We are listening only to gentle rushing waters. If an arm steals round a slender waist, what then? We are looking away to windward at the moonbeams on the sea. The gurgling ripples hide, perchance, the beating of two hearts which in the rush and clatter of the land would never have heard each other. Perhaps the mainsail conceals what the glare of a ball-room would have betrayed. . .

and so on, rhapsodically, until the boom goes over 'With a crash, and the lovers are rudely disturbed.' The dream is broken, concludes the author, 'but let us hope that the reality remains'. Let us hope they weren't in the way of the boom, either.

# 9108 HAVE YOU A LADY ON BOARD?

BUT TO MORE SERIOUS MATTERS. Every ship once had a permanent lady on board: its figurehead. Figureheads were as much part of a ship as curtains of a window: a vessel without one was unfinished, and that was that. Even HMS Warrior, the first iron-clad battleship in the Navy, was unbalanced in her trim by the addition of two tons of ornate carving, since John Scott Russell, her designer, opined that 'Jack Tar likes a figurehead'. Some were male, some political effigies, some animals: but the favourite figureheads were always women: nymphs, Venus, Amazons. Sometimes the Captain's wife would be depicted: many a North Country collier brig has a bluff bow surmounted by an equally bluff and plump little body in Early Victorian dress. They were usually carved to look pretty wind-swept: but one American clipper captain instructed that his figurehead should have her hair and draperies hanging quite still, without any suggestion of being blown backwards, because, he said 'I don't want my ship to look as if the wind is always dead ahead'.

This happy tradition was passed on to the

earlier 19th-century yachts, and some of the later ones; but by the onset of the First World War, they were a disappearing breed. The straight metal stem replaced the figure of romance. Very sad.

— **Have you a lady on board?** —

# 1297 ORDER A DONKEY TO BE GOT READY FOR THE LADY

BACK TO THE VOYAGE of the *Sunbeam*, with Lord Brassey and their vast entourage. Having nearly lost daughter Mabelle overboard to a freak wave ('She was perfectly self-possessed and only said "Hold on, Captain Lecky, Hold on" to which he replied "all right")' they boarded the wallowing wreck of the *Carolina* and looted it for some fine breakers of very new port, and then made into Funchal, Madeira. There were no donkeys to be had, but the dauntless ladies compromised on first a wicker sleigh pulled by two bullocks, and then (going down the mountain) a unique Madeira conveyance, a basketwork sleigh which bucketed down the tracks under the loose control of drivers who 'steer in the most wonderful manner down the zigzag road, making use of their bare feet as brakes where necessary. The only danger is the risk of fire from the friction of steel runners against the gravel road'.

# 9962 QUITE WORN OUT

If there is a languid tone to this final signal, it could be because not all these Victorian and Edwardian yachtowners were acting entirely out of personal enthusiasm for the sport. There were other things: status, family tradition, sheer habit. By the Edwardian era, even family tradition had got a bit diluted. One languid owner, when asked respectfully by his professional skipper whether he would like to take the helm, retorted 'I never take anything between meals'. Or consider Mr Herbert Weld, of Lulworth Castle. He took, we are told, a pride in continuing the Weld family tradition, but knew nothing much of seamanship. His yacht *Lulworth* won a good many races, but not usually due to any effort of his. The newspapers would be brought on board the yacht half an hour before the race started, and Weld would go below with *The Times* under his arm, and often not reappear until the race was well under way. 'Hullo!' he would say, casually looking around. 'We've started!'. His detachment caused considerable comment.

Still, perhaps Mr Weld was indeed Quite Worn Out: he was an explorer, archaeologist, naturalist and linguist, contributor to the British Museum and collector of 300 specimens of birds (including 17 new species) to the Natural History Museum. He had been a *Morning Post* correspondent in the South African War. One cannot help wondering why on earth he bothered to add yachting to his worries at all.

## Acknowledgments

This book was inspired by, and could not have been written without, research undertaken in the excellent Libraries of the National Maritime Museum, the Cruising Association and the Royal Cruising Club. Books of particular interest included *Memorials of the Royal Yacht Squadron* and *Further Memorials of the Royal Yacht Squadron*, by J B Atkins; *A Voyage in the Sunbeam* by Lady Brassey; *Sacred Cowes* by Anthony Heckstall-Smith; *Hunt-Room Stories* and *Yachting Yarns*, by 'Wanderer', *Salt Water Palaces* by Maldwin Drummond (Debrett), and *The Cumberland Fleet* by Douglas Phillips-Birt (The Royal Thames Yacht Club). All except these last two are, sadly, out of print.